PLACE

Jorie Graham is the author of twelve collections of poetry, including *The Dream of the Unified Field*, which won the Pulitzer Prize in 1996. She divides her time between western France and Cambridge, Massachusetts, where she teaches at Harvard University.

Also by Jorie Graham from Carcanet Press

Never
Swarm
The Errancy
The Dream of the Unified Field: Selected Poems 1974–1994
Overlord
Sea Change

PLACE

JORIE GRAHAM

CARCANET

First published in Great Britain in 2012 by Carcanet Press Limited
Alliance House
Cross Street
Manchester M2 7AQ

First published in the United States of America
by Ecco, an imprint of HarperCollins Publishers, 2012

A CIP catalogue record for this book is available from the British Library

ISBN 978 1 84777 193 3

The publisher acknowledges financial assistance from Arts Council England

Printed and bound in England by SRP Ltd, Exeter

for EMILY

Acknowledgments

Grateful acknowledgment to the editors of the journals and publications in which these poems first appeared:

The London Review of Books, The New Yorker, The Columbia Review, The Paris Review, The New Republic, The Paris Anthology, Fiddlehead Review (Canada), *The Boston Review, Lana Turner, Martha's Vineyard Arts & Ideas, A Public Space, Plume, EarthLines, The Cortland Review, The American Poetry Review.*

Thank you to the American Academy in Rome for time, and hospitality, which made much of this work possible.

CONTENTS

I

SUNDOWN

(St. Laurent Sur Mer, June 5, 2009)

Sometimes the day
                 light winces
                 behind you and it is
a great treasure in this case today a man on
                 a horse in calm full
                 gallop on Omaha over my
                 left shoulder coming on
                 fast but
calm not audible to me at all until I turned back my
                 head for no
                 reason as if what lies behind
                 one had whispered
what can I do for you today and I had just
                 turned to
                 answer and the answer to my
answer flooded from the front with the late sun he/they
                 were driving into—gleaming—
                 wet chest and upraised knees and
light-struck hooves and thrust-out even breathing of the great
                 beast—from just behind me,
                 passing me—the rider looking straight
                 ahead and yet
smiling without looking at me as I smiled as we
                 both smiled for the young
                 animal, my feet in the

breaking wave-edge, his hooves returning, as they begin to pass

        by,

        to the edge of the furling

        break, each tossed-up flake of

        ocean offered into the reddish

luminosity—sparks—as they made their way,

        boring through to clear out

        life, a place where no one

        again is suddenly

killed—regardless of the "cause"—no one—just this

        galloping forward with

        force through the low waves, seagulls

        scattering all round, their

screeching and mewing rising like more bits of red foam, the

        horse's hooves now suddenly

        louder as it goes

        by and its prints on

wet sand deep and immediately filled by thousands of

        sandfleas thrilled to the

declivities in succession in the newly

        released beach—just

        at the right

        moment for some

microscopic life to rise up through these

        cups in the hard upslant

        retreating ocean is

revealing, sandfleas finding them just as light does,

        carving them out with

        shadow, and glow on each

        ridge, and

water oozing up through the innermost cut of the

        hoofsteps,

and when I shut my eyes now I am not like a blind person

        walking towards the lowering sun,

the water loud at my right,

        but like a seeing person

with her eyes shut

        putting her feet down

        one at a time

        on the earth.

CAGNES SUR MER 1950

I am the only one who ever lived who remembers
my mother's voice in the particular shadow
cast by the skyfilled Roman archway
which darkens the stones on the down-sloping street
up which she has now come again suddenly.
How the archway and the voice and the shadow
seize the small triangle of my soul
violently, as in a silent film where the accompaniment
becomes a mad body
for the spirit's skipping images—abandoned homeland—miracle from which
we come back out alive. So here from there again I,
read it off the book of time,
my only time, as if in there is a fatal mistake of which
I cannot find the nature—or shape—or origin—I
pick up the infant and place it back again
to where I am a small reservoir of blood, twelve pounds of bone and
sinew and other matters—already condemned to this one soul—
which we are told weighs less than a feather, or as much
as four ounces when grown—as if I could travel, I back up
those arteries, up the precious liquid, across the field of methods, agonies,
astonishments—may I not squander the astonishments—
may I not mistakenly kill brother, sister—I
will sit once again so boldly at my beginning,
dark spot where one story does not yet become another,
and words, which have not yet come to me, will not yet try to tell
where each thing emerges, where it is heading,
and where the flow of tendency will shine

on its fast way downhill. And it will seem to me

that all this is legend,

one of those in which there is no way to look back

and yet you do, you pay for it, yes, but you do....

It was a hilltop town in the south in summer.

It was before I knew about knowing.

My mind ran everywhere and was completely still at the center.

And that did not feel uncomfortable.

A bird sang, it added itself to the shadow

under the archway.

I think from this distance

that I was happy.

I think from this distance.

I sat. It was before I knew walking.

Only my soul walked everywhere without weight.

Where the road sloped downhill there was disappearance.

Which was exactly what I imagined should happen.

Appearance and disappearance.

In my only life.

When my mother's voice got closer it had a body.

It had arms and they were holding something

that must have been a basket. My mind now

can go round her, come in front, and wrap her

as her arms wrapped that basket.

And it must have been wicker

because I see in the light the many lucent browns, the white tips,

as she steps out of the shadow

in which nothing but her hands and the front of her act of carrying

are visible. And when her body arrives

it is with the many lemons entirely struck, entirely taken, by sunshine,

which the heavy basket is still now carrying,

and her bright fingernails woven into each other,

and her face with its gaze searching for me,

gaze which felt like one of the bright things she was carrying
in front of herself, a new belly.
All I was to invent in this life is there in the wicker basket among the lemons
having come from below the horizon where the sound of the market rises
up into the private air in which she is moving,
where she is still a whole woman, and a willing woman,
and I hear what must be prices and names called out
of flowers and fruit and meat and live animals in small cages,
all from below us, at the bottom of the village, from that part
which is so comfortable to me which is invisible,
and in which everything has to be sold by noon.
I think that was the moment of my being given my name,
where I first heard the voices carrying the prices
as her face broke and its smile appeared bending down towards me
saying *there you are, there you are.*

MOTHER AND CHILD
(THE ROAD AT THE EDGE OF THE FIELD)

The grasses midsummer eve when the stems grow invisible and the

seemingly de-

capitated heads like a flock

that is not in the end departing but is lingering, golden with

buttery flies then also aglow with

orange—gnats

hovering their tiny solar system round—heads

bending this way and that in

unison glowing and not

showing where they

are attached to earth or what path has brought them to their

status; they for whom stasis

when it comes is the huge

inholding of breath by the whole

world as it is seen to be here, horizon to horizon stilling,

down to this corner field of grasses

held, bees all molten

with approach and with-

drawal—though of course there are still stars—albeit now in-

visible—and I look up into the

sky to see

beyond the foaming of

day's end the place where all in fact

is, longed-for or over-

looked altogether by the mind,

human, which can,

if it wishes,

ken them into view

by imagination—there is no invention—or not—as long as it

exists, the mind can

do this —

how many are the years you have

say the grass-pointings

which if I follow them up

and up

make of my eyeing large spidery webtrails into

the galaxy thank

god, and all that outlives

for sure the me in

me—a whirling robe humming with firstness greets you if you eye-up, confess it—

in letters home you would

tell this whole story but

nothing happened—the world opened its robe

and you

were free to look with

no sense of

excitement, no song, it is so simple, your lungs afloat, your

shears still there in your right

hand, the hedgerow wild beside you and how you can—yes—hear it

course up through its million

stalks—and also, closely

now, the single

skinny stalk—and how it is

true, all *is* being sucked up by the soil into the sky, and the sky

back down into variegation and

forking and fingery

elaboration at the core of prior

elaboration—spotted, incandescent—each about to be cast off by the one coming

behind—it too shall

contribute

to the

possible—the world of the world—and the shears

in my right hand grow warm

with the sun they've been hanging in, and I talk to myself, I make

words that follow from other

words, they push from be-

hind—into the hedge like the

hedge but not of it—no—not

ever—slippery against it where it

never knows they are pressing, delirious accents trying to reach in, fit

in—phantoms—as the calls

of the disappeared in the stadiums today are in-

audible, the satellite's announcement

of capture inaudible, the occupation of an

other's body, taken from its

private life its bed its

window its still half-open

fridge, dragged down the stairs with everyone

screaming—have you visited your

loved ones

recently says the guard as he lets loose the filamentary

shock of electricity through the body to the

heart whose words

will now

cease—what is cruelty—the grasses lean

all one way now under the sway of

difference, which evening's drop of

temperature brings on,

which the guard and the prisoner feel as one,

grassheads like spume on the thin shanks

of stalk—their until-now right there

beneath them—*grass,* I say,

grass, and rip a piece to hold out to you

who stand beneath me not yet speaking—everyone awaits

your first word—and I open your hand

and put the heads inside it and close it and I watch

terror spray from you in

colonies of tiny glances—everywhere but where

your hand is, and then

stalk I say, *poppy, thorn, hedgerose*—I am

not screaming because I am

old enough to hang on hang on

but your small heart beating as of two years now hears the

cannibalizing scream in all

my kindness—the mother

stands beside you and she sees you stare at her and put

your arm down and open your

fist and we both see the seeds drop

down onto the asphalt and the ground-breeze drag them

a little distance

to the middle

of the road

then stop. It is summer. It is the solstice. A diamond of energy

holds us. We breathe, and

what we call

the next moment between us,

where I take your empty hand and

we start home,

emptied of attempt and emptied of

survival skill,

is *love.*

UNTITLED

Of the two dogs the car hit, one, two, while we were talking, and thinking about

       how to change each

       other's

mind, the other people's

       survived—dark spot near the front

       fender just hair blowing in low wind, a spot all wind's, then

a stir in the ribs and everything's rising slow-motion up from the tight small shoulders, the

       chest, the

       dragging hind end of itself on the dirt

       road as if sewing a new strap

       back

on, dragging, a long

       moment, then the

       division occurs and the wide perishing shrinks and the legs

       are four again and

       up. Not ours. Ours

is placed by gravity on the far bank, as if an as-yet-unbuilt unimagined house on the

       empty field into which

       one peers past mist

       wondering how *will* or

concentration or *want* alone will bring the as-yet-not thing into view. What will it take to

       build the

       thing? The not yet, not anymore, not

       again? That. Wouldn't the beautiful field be best left

alone? unfilled? No. Now the children are folding

       over it and sound

       is restored and it is the only human

world, something perished on the road, it was its turn, you have your turn says the road I

stare blankly

at, white dust,

thinking there are words now

that must take the

place of this

creature, and I

am at the point in the road where I, who will have lived, no matter how many thousands

of years in the future come, if they come,

even if there are no more humans then or they have become unrecognizable, I,

even when no rain will have come down

in the memory of generations

so they think the story of such an element is one of the myths, the empty

myths, I still will have

lived this day and all the preceding ones of my

person, mine, as I rise now

to the moment when right words

are needed—Dear moon

this morning I woke up, I thought the room for an instant was a blossoming, then a

burning cell, then a thing

changing its clothes, huge transparent clothes, the ceiling part of the neck, where is

the head I thought, of the year, this

year, where are the eyes of

the years—the years, can we stay human, will we slow the end

down, how much, what do we have to promise, how think our way

from here to

there—and human life survived—and its world—ah, room, the

words—has it been just

luck, the room now wild with winds of centuries swirling floods tectonic plates like wide

bones shifting round me—elephants flow through, all gone, volcanoes emerging and

disappearing just like that, didn't even really get to see them, pestilence, there, it took its

people, hurricane, there,

it took its—"you're a

martian" I heard the angry child cry out on the street

below to the other

child, and the door slams, and the only story I know, my head, my century, the one where

187 million perished in wars, massacre, persecution, famine—all policy-induced—is the

one out of which

I must find the reason

for the loved still-young creature being carried now onto the family lawn as they try

everything, and all murmurs shroud hum cry instruct, and all the

six arms gleam, firm, limp, all over it, caresses, tentacular

surround of the never-again, rush of blood and words, although look, you out there

peering in, listening, to see who we were: here: this was history:

their turn

is all they actually have

flowing in them.

THE BIRD ON MY RAILING

From

the still wet iron of

my fire

escape's top

railing a truth is making this instant on our clock

open with a taut

unchirping un-

breaking note—a perfectly

released vowel traveling

the high branches across the way, between us and the

others, in their

apartments, and fog

lifting for sun before evaporation

begins. Someone

is born

somewhere

now. The

planet

suspends

like a streetlight

at night

in the quiet

galaxy.

Endurance

continues to be the secret of the tilled

ground we make

breath by breath. What

seed dear

lord are we we

think as we toss more of our living out

into the turning and turning,

our personal

dead cast always deeper into

the general dead

no matter how hard you try

to keep your

own your

known own—and gnarled remembering mossing over—

the tenderness a characteristic trait

elicits, the very thing you

hated, rising in you to

make you almost

unable to

speak—

—where *are* you?—the fields beyond the housing tract

still accepting rain

as these asphalted ones we've

sealed

cannot—so yes, look close, this right word on my railing

who knows no hate

no love

you can count on it,

no wrenching strangling guilt, no wish so terrible

one had said

otherwise just once in

time—

between one life and another what is it that

can really

exist—oh

nothing says this

awakeness—and look, you

             who might not believe this because

you are not seeing it with your own

             eyes: look:

             this light

             is moving

             across that flower on

             my sill

             at this exact

speed—right now—right here—now it is gone—yet go back up

             five lines it is

             still there I can't

             go back, it's

             gone,

             but you—

what is it you are

             seeing—see it again—a yellow

             daisy, the sun

             strafing the petals once

across, and the yellow, which could be a god why not,

             pulling itself up

             out of

shadow—so

             silent—

             and the patch of sunlight

             moves—and each word said in

             time after this is

             the subtraction we call

life-lived—this gold its center—and beyond it, still on

             the rail, this

             bird, a

             secret gift to

             me by the

             visible—

of which few in a life are

        given—and how

        when it opens its

        yellow beak in the glint-sun to

        let out song

        into the cold, it

lets out the note on a plume of

        steam,

        lets out the

        visible heat of its

        inwardness

carrying a note—a note in

        a mist—a note-

        breath, breath-

        note—oh

cold spring—the white

        plume the size of a

        bird rises up with its own

        tail,

        feathering-out in

the directions,

        filled out by the next and the next-on

        note, until the whole

        shape of the

        song is wisped-

        up and

shuts,

        the singing

        shuts, the form

        complete, the breath-bird

        free to

        rise away into the young day and

not be—

II

END

(November 21, 2010)

End of autumn. Deep fog. There are chains in it, and sounds of
                              hinges. No that was
                              birds. A bird and a
                              gate. There are
swingings of the gate that sound like stringed
                              instruments from
                              some other
                              culture. Also a
hammering which is held

                              in the fog
                              and held. Or it is continuing to
                              hammer. I hear the blows.
Each is distant so it seems it should not repeat. It repeats. What is it being hammered
                              in. Fog all over the
                              field. The sounds of
                              boots
on soil in groups those
                              thuds but then it is
                              cattle I
                              think. The sound of the hinge the swinging chain it won't
go away. But it is just the farmer at work. He must be putting out
                              feed. Fog. Play at
                              freedom now it

says, look, all is

blank. Come to the

front, it is

your stage it

says, the sound of the clinking of links of

chain, I think it is someone making the chain—*that* is the hammering—the thuds—making

their own chain. But no, it is the gate and the herd is let in again, then

out. I can hear

the mouths eating, dozens maybe hundreds, and the breathing in and out as they

chew. And the

chain. For now I am alive I think into the hammering

thudding clinking swinging of metal hinge—of hinge—and also think maybe this is

winter now—first day of. Fog and a not knowing of. Of what. What is inner

experience I think being

shut out. I look. A gate swings again and a rustling

nearby. All is

nearby and invisible. The clinking a chinking of someone making nails. The sounds of a crowd

meaning to be silent, all their breathing. Having been told not to move and to be

silent. Then having been told to

move and be

silent. The crowd is in there. All the breaths they are trying

to hold in, make

inaudible. And scraping as of metal on metal, and dragging as of a heavy thing. But it is a field

out there. My neighbor has his herd on it. When I walk away from the

window it's a violin I

hear over the

chewing out of tune torn string but once it made

music it might still make

music if I become a new way of

listening, in which

above all,

nothing, I know nothing, now there are moans

out there such as a man accused and tossed away by his fellow beings, an aloneness, and

listen, it is blank but in it is an

appeal, a ruined one, reduced, listen: in

there this

animal

dying slowly

in eternity its

trap.

ON THE VIRTUE OF THE DEAD TREE

And that you hold the same one hawk each day I pass through my field

up. And that it

may choose its

spot so

freely, from which to scan, and, without more than the wintry beguiling

wingstrokes seeding

the fields of air,

swoop. It feeds. There is no wasteland where the dead oak

lives—my

darling—up-

start vines on its trunk, swirling in ebblight, a desert of gone-silent

cells—where another force is

gleaming—tardy—

waning—summer or winter no longer

truths, no prime, no

year, no day where sun

exists—

just a still-being-here in this small apparently silent multitudinous world of

infinite yearning and

killing and

sprouting—even now at the very start of the season—lengthening, in-

visible in their

cracking open of

pod—and push—like the first time we saw each other you and I—

impatient immediately . . .

Blackness is the telephone wire—blackness the blissless instant-

communication,

the twittering poverty killing behind and beneath and deep at the core of

each screen, end-

less, someone breaking someone's

fingers—just now—hear their laughter—everyone in their prison—there in their human

heart which

they cannot

for all the parting of flesh with

cement-sluiced rubber

hose—and even the axe to the heart—reach—the fantasy of independence—es-

cape. It wants them. It wants them to

fly inside it. *Fly* it screams

taser in

hand. Prison is never

going to be

over. Day as it breaks is the principal god, but with the hood on they cannot

know this. Till it is finally sliced open the

beating heart. Loved

ones shall pay

ransom

for the body of

their child. To this, friend, the hero is the dead tree. Here in my field, mine.

I have forced it. I have paid for it. My money like a wind flowing over it.

Have signed the paperwork and seen my name there. And a cloud

arrives from the East

into it. And the prison

grows too large to see.

And it does not sing, ever,

my silent hawk, always there when I arrive, before it startles, on its chosen

branch. And I think of

the dead-through trunk, the leafless limbs, the loosening of the

deep-drying roots in the

living soil. And I slow myself to extend love to them. To their as-

yet-still-sturdy

rotting, and how they hold

up this gray-blue

poverty of once-sapflowing

limbs, their once everywhere-turning

branchings,

for my small hungry creature to glide from in his silence

over the never-for-an-instant-not-working

rows of new

wheat. It is

good says my human soul to the crop. I will not listen for

song anymore. I will

listen for how dark comes-on to loosen the cringing wavering

mice from their dens and

how they creep up to the surfaces and out onto the surfaces and

how the surfaces

yield their small gray velvet barely visible in the last glow

to that part of the world

the dead tree sends forth. I have lived I

say to the evening.

I have plenty of anger and am good and dry with late-breaking news. I

am living.

And the iron door of the night creeps and clicks. And the

madness of the day

hangs around restless at the edges of the last visible leaves

with a reddish glow

and moves them with tiny

erratic swiftnesses and

the holy place shuts, baggy with evening, and here it is

finally night

bursting open

with hunt.

DIALOGUE
(OF THE IMAGINATION'S FEAR)

All around in

        houses near us, the

        layoffs,

        the windows shine back

        sky, it is a

        wonder we

can use the word *free* and have it mean anything at all

        to us. We stand still. Let the cold wind wrap round go

        into hair in-

between fingers. The *for sale* signs are bent and ripple in

        wind. One

had fallen last Fall and snowmelt is re-revealing

        it again. Rattle in groundwind. Siding

        weakening on

        everything. Spring!

        Underneath

        the bulbs want to clear the sill of

        dark and find the

        sun. I see

        them now

under there, in there, soggy with melt, and loam which is loosening as their skins

rot, to let the whitest tendrils out, out they go snaking everywhere, till the

        leaves are blurring, they fur-out, they

        exist!—

        another's year loan

        to time—

and the bud will form in the sleeve of the silky leaf, and they will quietly,
among the slow working pigeons and there where a dog is leaping in almost
                              complete invisibility, make slim heads,
                              thicken—I am ill, you know, says the man walking by,
his dog pulling him, so much joy, and nothing
                              will make it more or less, the flower,
as alive as it is dead, above which the girl with earphones walks humming, no one
                              has warned her yet she is
                              free, but why, says the
                              imagination, have you sent me
                              down here, down among the roots, as they finally take
hold—it is hard—they wrench, the loam is not easy to open, I cannot say it but the
smell is hope meeting terrifying regret, I would say do not open again, do not go up,
                              stay under here there is
                              no epoch, we are
                              in something but it is not "the world," why try to make
                              us feel at
                              home down
                              here, take away the poem, take away this desire that
has you entering this waste dark space, there are not even pockets of time here,
there are no mysteries, there is no laughter and nothing ever dies, the foreclosure
                              you are standing beside look to it, there is a
woman crying on the second floor as she does not understand what it will be like to
not have a home now, and how to explain to the children at 3:35 when the bus drops
                              them off—
the root is breaking its face open and shoving up to escape
                              towards
                              sun—nothing can stop it—though right
now the repo-men have not yet come, the school bus is only just getting loaded up,
the children pooling squealing some stare out the window. Kiss
                              the soil as you
pass by. It is coming up to kiss you. Bend down to me, you have placed me here, look
to me on all fours, drink of the puddle, look hard at the sky in there. It is not sky. It is

not there. The flame of

sun which will come out just now for a blinding minute

into your eyes is saving nothing, no one, take your communion, your blood is full of

barren fields, they are the

future in you you

should learn to feel and

love: there will be no more: no more: not enough to go around: no more around: no

more: love that.

EMPLOYMENT

Listen the voice is American it would reach you it has wiring in its swan's neck
where it is
always turning
round to see behind itself as it has no past to speak of except some nocturnal
journals written in woods where the fight has just taken place or is about to
take place
for place
the pupils have firelight in them where the man a surveyor or a tracker still has
no idea what
is coming
the wall-to-wall cars on the 405 for the ride home from the cubicle or the corner
office—how big
the difference—or the waiting all day again in line till your number is
called it will be
called which means
exactly nothing as no one will say to you as was promised by all eternity "ah son, do you
know where you came from, tell me, tell me your story as you have come to this
Station"—no, they
did away with
the stations
and the jobs
the way of
life
and your number, how you hold it, its promise on its paper,
if numbers could breathe each one of these would be an
exhalation, the last breath of something
and then there you have it: stilled: the exactness: the number: your

number. That is why they

can use it. Because it was living

and now is

stilled. The transition from one state to the

other—they

give, you

receive—provides its shape.

A number is always hovering over something beneath it. It is

invisible, but you can feel it. To make a sum

you summon a crowd. A large number is a form

of mob. The larger the number the more

terrifying.

They are getting very large now.

The thing to do right

away

is to start counting, to say it is my

turn, mine to step into

the stream of blood

for the interview,

to say I

can do it, to say I

am not

one, and then say two, three, four and feel

the blood take you in from above, a legion

single file heading out in formation

across a desert that will not count.

TREADMILL

The road keeps accepting us. It wants us to learn "nowhere," its shiny
                        emptiness, its smile of wide days, so swollen
with void, it really means it, this is not a vacation, it wants us
                        to let our skulled-in mind, its channels and runnels, its
                        slimy stalked circuits, connecting wildly, it the road
                        wants us
                        right now
                        to cast it the
                        mind
                        from its encasement
                        forward
to race up ahead and get a feel for what it is, this always-receding, this place in which
                        you were to deposit your
                        question—the
                        destination!—the mind is meant to want this, isn't it,
                        meant to rage to
                        handle it, to turn it
                        round, to feel
                        all its
                        facets—its fine
                        accidents—death by water, death by
wearing out—death by surprise—death by marriage—death by having rummaged
into the past, into the distant past—death by ice-core and prediction—the entrails are lying on a
thousand years of tabletops—have you not looked into them enough says the grayish
                        road, hissing, or maybe
                        that is my mind, I
                        entered the poem here,

on line 28, at 6:44 pm, I had been trying to stay outside, I had not wanted to
put my feet here too, but the wind came up, a little achilles-wind, the city itself took
time off from dying to whisper into my ear we need you, the complaint which we will
nail once again to the door must be signed by everyone, everyone needs to be walking
together, everyone must feel the dust underfoot, death by drought, death by starvation,
death by neglect, death by no cause of death, by unfolding—oh the rose garden—
dew still on it, the dry fields in each drop held up by the petal—look you can see
the cracks in the soil reflected right there—puritanical dried fields—sincerity at utmost
in the fissured field—the screen is empty—is full of cracked soil—the soil—
death by transcendent truth—death by banking practice—by blueprint and mutually
assured destruction—death by deterrent—detergent—derangement—defamation—de-
regulation—the end of the line—where the tracks just stop and
who is that coming from the woodshed to greet you—the end is always cheerful
                says the day hurrying alongside as you splice
                through it, as you
                feel your astonishing aloneness grow funnily
                winged—who are you going to be
someday, who are you going to be when all this clay flowing through you has
                finally become
                form, and you catch a glimpse of yourself at daybreak,
                there in the shiny broken-faced
                surface—
who was awaiting you all day that you hurried so—what was it you were told to
                accomplish—death, rimless stare, O, hasn't enough time
passed by now, can the moving walkway be shut down for the night, but no,
                it is told, it is told, the universe
                is in your mind as it
                expands—and it is October once again
as it must be, the new brightness—
                and again gold lays down on them
                the tight rolls of hay,
                the long rows the cut fields—
which Winter eyes, hidden as it is at the core of everything, and the crows sharpen

their blade-calls on the morning,

and frost blooms its parallel world,

and the road seems to want to be spooled into your hands, into your mind, fine

yarn you would ravel

back to its place of

origin—

is it true some people are not coming along with us? is it really true there is

a road not taken? and it is October once again

as it must be, the new brightness, the harvest—the dance—

and your dance partner, be prudent, it

really knows the

steps.

III

OF INNER EXPERIENCE

Eyes shut I sense I am awakening & then I am

        awake but

        deciding

to keep eyes shut, look at the inside, stay inside, in the long and dark of it,

          if it were a garden what would I plant

          in it, for now I am

alive I think I feel who among you will tell me

        after all this time

the difference & yet again now I am alive & what does that mean lying here eyes

          closed first winter morning coming on all round,

          yes, this is the start of winter is what

          my body

          sensing a new dis-

equilibrium says, hypnotized, trembling with fiction, love, the sensation of time passing,

          & fear of a-

          temporality, & *this is*

          the play of heaven the mind in-

          side this body lying here still

          alive for

          now

thinks—if you could only see my body and beyond me the three windows in the room

          letting the uninvented

          in—and how true *it* is

          because of the closed

eyes on my human being lying there in the room glistening with plenitude, all conquest

gone from the air—you could say here god owns everything, it is a discharge of duration,

the floor the panes the mirror the single stalk of
freesia the gilded frame the two lionclaw-footed chairs and the tree-knots
still in
the floors someone laid in 1860, the
wormholes here and there in them from those creatures' work long ago, not long after the
counter-revolution, the troubles—& the wreck here of consciousness—as long as the
person's eyes
stay shut—beyond the limits of thought—(& who am I
then?)(& don't go there says my hand as I need it, my
hand, here in this
writing)—and yet
I am also lying on the bed eyes closed
and keeping them so, god owes us
everything I
think from out here, there is not god I think lying in the non-dark of the mind, eyes
closed, hearing the crows rustling in
the nearest
trees, the hayfork in the next field—I want to pray says the person behind the eyes—you

cannot do so I say with these fingers—I want to break the dark with the idea of God says the

non-sleeping person on her back in the beginning of the 21st century, trying to hold on to

duration which is slipping, slipping, as she speaks as I write, active translator, look
I can make a tale of the sinking sun I can begin
summer again here are its
swallows they have
just returned
look
up—but no, they did not come back after that year, we waited—but here they
are again, do not be
fooled, here, breaking their circles
across the evening air, and there is still sun up near the children's bedtime, we still say

bedtime, it is a habit, and the bells
ring vespers, or the recording of it, and somewhere there must still be a crafty
animal digging a long tunnel under
this strange hard ground, finding some moisture in there, turning it, grain by grain,
perhaps there is still
the creature
which when it
was known
was known as
the blind mole
somewhere.

TORN SCORE

I think this is all somewhere inside myself, the incessant burning of my birth

all shine

lessening as also all low-flame

heat of

love: and places loved: space time and people heightening, burning, then nothing:

always less

incipience as visible

time shows itself—the

stamens the groves the winds their verdicts the walls and the other walls behind,

also the

petal right now off that red

amaryllis, then stillness, then one awaiting the next thing of each thing, a needle

trembling in a

hand, dust

settling on the apple tree, the last bus out no longer held in memory by anyone

among the living, the last

avenues of

poplars

downed, and the bow raised

just where the violinist inhales and begins to lower it, the lucent string, and in
the audience everything—everything—the lovers the suicides the broken brothers
the formless the suffocating the painstakingly decent the young-for-eternity the
gods, those with sharpened knives even now in their hearts, those with pennies,
theories, history, simplicity, drink—perpetually—please music begin, the years are
disappearing, no one will cough, the listening is of a piece—a desperate fabric—
artificial fire, violin, begin, faithful to the one truth, precision, utterly, begin—who

shut the lights, who burned the scores, broke all the

        instruments—I see the pieces on the road—

        this world that

        was, just minutes ago, the only one that

        was—you're in it

        now—say *yes*

        out loud—say am I a

        personal

wholeness? a congerie of chemical elements? of truths held self-

        evident?—how do I see them?—to be alive,

        is it

        to be

        faithful? to be

an arch, a list, a suddenly-right second-thought? a potential? a law that would like

        goodness built

        into

        its

        constitution—a game

        of sorts—a

friend—one who rebukes impatience—foundational—unapathetic—attracted to the

subject of life, all accounts of it, a presence of the human so real you will

        believe in me?—

are you still there, where I was looking a minute ago—how long that

        minute—the dangers then were

        broken law or

        lock or

        heart—a broken

        seal, code, word, train

        of

        thought—what, we thought, should we be

        capable of

        to cross

time—to be a good

animal? even

sacrificial?—and then, looking up now, oh,

blurred small all at once dropping

quick deadweight then

winged and

up, then

hopping—float, hover, hover—then

down

to the small

melt-pool, in which the

unbegun budless trees at attention

glitter, and my

attention,

so hungry not to slip out of its

catch, its span—held

breath—hovers—

those could be last fall's leaves piled on dead leaves, thinning, trans-

lucent, but

they are feathers,

look close,

specked,

coming loose from

snow and rushing now, all of them at once now, down, into the branchfilled glassy

pool of sky to

thrash apart

small cheeping birds, all appetite—

THE SURE PLACE

Outside the window this morning, I reach to it, the newest
extension, here at second story, of the wisteria vine—
the tenth summer's growth,
the August 13th portion of,
the rootball planted when still
the mother of a new child,
one almost tired-looking very silent out-arriving
tendril—what kind of energy is this in my hands,
this tress of glucose and watery scribbling—something which cannot reach
conclusion, my open palm just under it,
the outermost question being asked me by the world today—
it is weak it is exactly the right weakness—
we have other plans for your life says the world—
wind coming from below with the summery tick in it,
where it rounds and tucks-up from fullness where it allows one to hear
the rattling in the millions of now-drying seedpods
hanging in the trees off the walls under the hedges,
every leaf has other plans for you say the minutes also the seconds also the tiniest
fractions of whatever atoms make this a hot breezeless day,
in which what regards the soul is what it has given back
(when the sky is torn)(when the seas are poured forth)
the wisteria in my hand: who made it, who made it right,
what does it know of the day of reckoning, is today its day—
I could pull it, my vine, down, I could rip it out—still
no day of reckoning—the day it is said when no soul
can help another—each is alone—the unseen will say do not hoard me—
do not—as I hold its tether in the morning-light slant—

as the horizon does not seem to hoard the unseen—

so also the ideas are not emptied, look I am holding one—

shall we say that this instant is the end of time

where I raise my hand into the advancing morning

where the dawn-cool lifts to let the stillness of midday be seen

here underneath these low-flowing mists

which all the long time are still and waiting

for that one heat that will not change its face,

even when the horsemen ride up and it is time, and the face of the heat

stays, shimmers-stays, and the knives of the day turn blade-out

in the long corridor of noon which comes looking for this tendril—

and I hold it tight to the stone

as I bring the string round it

not to crush the sucrose and glucose in it but still

to hold it back that the as yet unformed blossoms

that would channel up it might channel up it

coming finally to spawn in long grapelike drooping

which the bees next month—what is that—will come to inhabit,

a slowness which is exactly the right slowness,

and I tell you I can feel in it that one crisp thought

which I must find a way to fix

upon this wall, driving a nail in now, and then a length of string,

around which to wrap this new growth, for it to cling to and surpass

so that next week when I look again it will have woven round its few more times

and grown hairy in its clinging and gotten to a new length

which we will be called upon to tie back, new knot, new extension,

to the next-on nail yet further up

on what remains on what's left of this wall.

ALTHOUGH

Nobody there. The vase of cut flowers with which the real is (before us on this page)

      permeated—is it a page—look hard—(I try)—this bouquet

      in its

vase—tiger dahlias (red and white), orange freesia (three stalks) (floating

      out), one

      large blue-mauve hydrangea-head, still

      wet (this

bending falling heavy with

      load) (and yellow

      rose)

(wide open head, three just-slitting buds) (also holding drops of rain)

      each at

diagonal, urchins in sea-sway, this

      from the real, which the real may continue (who can know

      this) to

      hold, this

      of which

      the real is

      just now

      made—blue-green glazed

vase on the worn wood table—oak with water stains

      from where the rain sweeps sideways

      in the wind

      though today it is dry

      reflected in this mirror hung outdoors,

      under a roofed

alcove, the field in it also, the trees so still one imagines as one always did they are almost

sentient,

and beyond that the steeple,

if you were alive you could put your finger

to the spot on the glass

where the village's buildings begin, then glide it over to the front-most

salmon rose,

the one with a blot of rain still on the inner lip, in a world where someone else could still

hold you, or hold you in mind,

or be coming to get you soon,

or soon

could be there, the "soon," the someone

"else," the instants as they crept upon us, the green beyond the terrace now

also in there—but what

is it that is

in there, in the glass, pocked where the

mercury backing cracks, there yet not

being penetrated by

a human gaze, nobody there,

the distant treetops in the evening sky, not there, though flashing,

pierced full of pinprick holes the sky not

there, the present

being elsewhere, you can almost rub elbows with it, you, not there,

this was the day it happened you say

down on your knees

though only in your head

a head not really anywhere as this is happening

after the fact

when nobody is anywhere, not anymore, but of so recent

date, this final absence, that the bouquet—roses, freesia, hydrangea, dahlia—oranges and

pinks and mossy greens—has sun still all soaked up in it, the cells in stalks still

sucking water up,

the ends still reaching it to feed,

cut ends, what someone had cut, had re-

arranged, seen to the placement of, in such a way

as the back and front are simultaneously visible,

because of the mirror,

on this terrace wall,

so things are coming at you as they leave,

and leaving from you as they come,

but there is no one in the glare of day,

is there still day, one of the days, are there still "ones" of

things—vases or days—

you think it is wrong, perhaps, to play this game

when we are all

still here,

then just on time, the dawn, piling itself on all the previous dawns,

on your head on your back on your shut eyes,

one after the other, each with a number and with only

that number—

lays itself down,

like a load

delivered, an invisible face adding itself to the huge

crowd of faces,

staring at you,

each one your next day,

it makes no difference if the lightning goes crazy if the wind

accomplishes

everything

it wishes to accomplish and you are

afraid—listen—the dogs bark—but where?—

the irregularity of your breath

next to the next person's

breathing—oh—

we turned away during the parade—

we looked above the heads of the performers to the

"whole" as we called it,

or to the *idea* it also

was, yes, but

it wanted only to be seen and heard and for you to stand hard

and see the raveling

of the minutes

incarnate

in event—and now, now, all this fidelity

is asked

of you

to the stage-set. . . .

A long period of adjustment must follow.

We must write the history of time.

We must put the children under the tree

again, and in their hearts the wiring, so green.

We must write the history of appearances

that tomorrow be invested

with today

as casually as the conversation drifting in from the next

room,

hard facts being reported in a calm voice,

the world a place we got use out of,

we must write of the use we got

of it—

the meaning not apparent ever, no matter what

you later on find of

our thinking—

but the fourth wall so clear

throughout the whole of human time.

How we came to keep living

but to no longer be

inhabitants.

IV

THE BIRD THAT BEGINS IT

In the world-famous night which is already flinging away bits of dark but not

        quite yet

        there opens

        a sound like a

        rattle, then a slicing in which even the

        blade is

audible, and then again, even though trailing the night-melt, suddenly, again, the

        rattle. In the

night of the return of day, of next-on time, of

        shape name field

        with history flapping

        all over it

invisible flags or wings or winds—(*victory* being exactly

        what it says,

        the end of night)

(it is not right to enter time it mutters as its tatters

        come loose)—in the

        return I

        think *I*

        am in this body—

I really only think it—this body lying here is

        only my thought,

        the flat solution

        to the sensation/question

        of

who is it that is listening, who is it that is wanting still

        to speak to you

out of the vast network

of blooded things,

a huge breath-held, candle-lit, whistling, planet-wide, still blood-flowing,

howling-silent, sentence-driven, last-bridge-pulled-up-behind city of

the human, the expense-

column of place in

place humming. . . . To have

a body. A borderline

of ethics and reason. Here comes the first light in leaf-shaped coins.

They are still being flung at our feet. We could be Judas no

problem. Could be

the wishing-well. Right

here in my open

mouth. The light can toss its wish right down this spinal

cord,

can tumble in

and buy a wakened self. . . . What is the job today my being

asks of

light. Please

tell me my job. It cannot be this headless incessant crossing

of threshold, it cannot be

more purchasing of more

good, it cannot be more sleeplessness—the necklaces of

minutes being tossed

over and over my

shoulders. The snake

goes further into the grass as

first light hits.

The clay

in the soil gleams where dew withdraws. Something we don't want

any more of

flourishes as never

before. I

      feel the gravity

      as I sit up

like a leaf growing from the stalk of the unknown

still lying there behind me where my sleep just was. Daylight

        crackles on the sill. Preparation

        of day

        everywhere

        underfoot. Across

the sill, the hero unfolding in the new light, the

        girl who would

        not bear the

        god a

son, the mother who ate her own grown

        flesh, the god

        who in exchange

for Time gave as many of his children as need be

        to the

        abyss. It is

        day.

The human does not fit in it.

LULL

At the forest's edge, a fox

                came out.

                It looked at

us. Nobody coming up the hill hungry looking

                to take

                food. The fox-

                eye

trained. Nobody coming up the

                hill in the broad

                daylight with an

                axe for

wood, for water, for the store in the

                pantry. I stock

                the pantry. I

watch for rain. For too much

                rain, too

                fast, too

                little, too

long. When dryness begins I hear the woods

                click. Unusual.

                I hear the arid. Un-

                usual. My father

                is dying of

age, good, that is usual. My valley is,

                my touch, my sense, my law, my

                soil, my sensation of

                my first

person. Now everything is clear. Facts lick their tongue deep

      into my ear.

Visiting hour is up. We are curled

      on the hook we placed in our brain and down

      our throat into our

      hearts our inner

      organs we

      have eaten

the long fishing line of the so-called journey and taken its

      fine piercing into

      our necks backs hands it comes out our

mouths it re-enters our ears and in it goes

      again deep the dream

      of ownership

we count up everyone to make sure we are all here

      in it

      together, the only

      share-

holders, the applause-lines make the

      tightening line

      gleam—the bottom line—how much

      did you think you

      could *own*—the first tree

we believed was a hook we got it

      wrong—the fox is still

      standing there it

      is staring it is

not scared—there is nothing behind it, beyond it—no value—

      the story of Eden:

      revision: we are now

breaking into the Garden. It was, for the

      interglacial lull,

      protected

from

us now we

have broken

in—have emptied all

the limbs the streaming fabric of

light milliseconds leaves the now inaudible

birds whales bees—have

in these days made arrangements to get

compensation—from what

we know not but the court says

we are to be

compensated

for our way of life being

taken from us—fox says

what a rough garment

your brain is

you wear it all over you, fox says

language is a hook you

got caught,

try pulling somewhere on the strings but no

they are all through you,

had you only looked

down, fox says, look down to the

road and keep your listening

up, fox will you not

move on my heart thinks checking the larder the

locks fox

says your greed is not

precise enough.

WAKING

(Ecrammeville, 6 A.M.)

The bells again. You open up your eyes
                again. A gap. To be a person—
human and then a woman.
                To be one who has had
                enough.
Enough of the basement.
                Enough of the garden
with its high wall though not high enough with all
                the spy-holes unless they were
                just accidental cracks
                through which one could see
the world. It took myth to get one's self
                out. It took
                a vow
to believe in a
                god
                to get the courage to
                get out.
Of what? World, you hunger with a briefcase
                running through the streets
                quickly hiding those hands
wanting to *feel* something: the bells
                ring as they do, one long note, one
short, a man with a tall hood limping and
                limping and yet always staying

in place I

think

listening. It does not go forward or up or down this

call to

prayer, a creature stuck in a doorway

made to cough up

one truth

without alteration. It will not

confess to

anything. The thing the bell is

saying stays for its millennia

the same, dripping in flames, in holy

men, in

cries and rage of

why yet another son

for no reason with his raw soul has to be

ripped from

time—so commonplace the pain—

& you are supposed to make a system

of them—all those

the god loves and wants

to take a closer look at, ex-

amine in

detail,

entrail and eye, kneecap in left hand, earlobe in

right, I see him look from

one to the

other then

bend down to pick up hair and these few fingers—see—

he does not know where they

must go—maybe in

this chick of hair—his left hand moving to his

right, carrying fingers, nails,

into the hair but then

something is

not right—he tries the eyes in the

palm of a

hand, tries eyes

into an open woman's

sex, tries many eyes, tries them in

mouth but mouth

has no face, ribs in one hand,

calves with heavy feet still on in

other—looks

dismayed—looks affronted—it will not make

its sense

to him

its maker—no—

quickly he shuts the whole pile back into the bloody sack

and tosses it

aside to where it seems its people hope (he can

hear them) (therefore the bells) its people

on their knees now

hope—their person is being judged—and they make

offerings, and they re-

member all

the best

parts, all,

and they begin

to sing.

They give him everything they have. They sing.

THE FUTURE OF BELIEF

(On Parcel Z 52 in the Purchase and Sale Agreement)

There are things you have to put into a face.

There it is hanging before you lips slightly parted.

It is not going to speak get over it it is not.

But it is not shut. No. There are things you must put into it—

you cannot arrive blind at your destination—nor can you carry the load

all the way—thus the face—and its hollow—awaiting your history—it is a box a dream a

cage a cellar an envelope a place a bomber hides while

waiting, a place a singer will kill his voice in order not to sing

for those who would make him cover up the

execution, a place where breath can be held only for

so long while the troops inspect the keep, the cough pushed

                        down so hard

into the throat that no sound give us up, yet how they keep on

searching, lingering, fiddling with this and that, how long, how long can it

be held, the small winged thing the cough the tickle of

death, just this side of surprise, could death be any smaller than it now

is, look, you can slide it into the face without the face even knowing it,

a wafer is thicker, an illusion is heavier, how long

can one stay behind one's face, eyes shut, as there are things

even a face cannot hold, but we are not there yet, there is still room here, there are still

                        things it must

be made to hold, the centuries, the theory of the original image of some

God, in its cave there are skirmishes, this one says you are my

archive, this other the brother says you must be my

safebox I have stolen a great many necessary things, also you

will be my confessional, I will put my story in you and you will cleanse it by listening, I will with feline

quickness shove my monologue into you, that it not be

fatal, into you, that I may step back and stare,

that I might see myself as on a visit to you.

I will put my hand in your mouth,

I will put my words in your eyes, don't recede don't shut,

I will put into you this distance spiked with gigantic summits I can't handle any more,

a place neither childhood nor future fill, a self-erasing page—watch

                                                      your target-

practice—the face might not need that bullet—look instead how this interested

glance comes into it—its hard bit of dust—see how this desiring gaze

agglomerates in it—scratching about to see what's

there—what's there?—a steeple has fallen in on a house, the face holds

the rubble so you can walk around in it without fear, you can search

the debris in it, don't worry about

time, you can check to see if the bodies still have pulse, you can remove their

documents, you can remove their tags, no one is shouting at you now,

elsewhere in the face the gleaming factory can be reached,

a thousand new planes line up for the inspection, you can watch

the finishing touches being given, you can see them

become operational, in the face, you just have to

look, also the one man in the overcoat

watching the men he just ordered to shoot

at the long row of humans

take aim in unison, the trees are also there, behind the ones about to be

killed, a pit has been dug along the tree line, some roots exposed now grayly gleam as

earliest light hits, and hold the shine while bodies start to slap down into

                                                     its bluish

soil, one can see clay in it, strata, also the snow from last night holding on,

the guns now lowered as this job is done,

forty seven portions of woolen clothing and skin

fed to the morning's ditch, ten of them ordered now

to close it up, this being put by these means into the face, here, open its eyes open its mouth, put it in, don't forget the plumes where the twenty rifles go off in unison,

which looks like a fluff of windy snow

where the bullets traverse the open space towards trees,

intercepted by the chests and faces of

the people standing there, you can put their muddy jackets and the shawls held tightly

round for

one last

instant now into the face, you can.

EARTH

Into the clearing shimmering which is my owned

                lawn between

                two patches of

                woods near

dawn clock running as usual the human in me

                watching as usual

                for

everything to separate from everything again as light

                comes back

                and the dark

which smothers so beautifully the earth lifts and all is put

                on its leash

                again one

                long leash

such as this sentence—and

                into the open beyond my window-

                pane the new

                day comes as if

                someone its constant

                master

calls—it never refuses, lingers, slows, it doesn't

                abandon us—and I see it, the planet, turn through the

                barely lifting latex

                shade, and the just-rising sunbeam-sliver like a nail-trim move

across the tree-grain on the floor across those hundreds of

                years of molecules

                sucking-in water and light—

                this slightly

C-shaped edge of the billion-light-year-toss-of-a-coin—

                        sometimes trembling a

                        bit if the shade

                        lets in wind—

                        inexorably—

and I see you my planet, I see your exact rotation now on my

                        floor—I will not close these eyes in this my

                        head lain

                        down on its

                        sheet, no, its

sleeplessness will watch, under room-tone,

                        and electromagnetism,

the calculations fly off your flanks as you

                        make your swerve,

                        dragging the increasingly

yellow arc across the room here

                        on this hill and

                        I shall say now

because of human imagination:

                        here on this floor this

                        passage is

                        your wing, is

                        an infinitesimal

                        strand of a feather in

                        your wing,

this brightening which does not so much move, as

                        the minute hand

                        near my eye

                        does, as it

glides—a pulling as much as a pushing—of event—

                        so that you are never

                        where you just were and yet

                        my eye has not

moved, not truly, is staying upon your back and riding you—

I don't want the moon and the stars, I want to lie here arms

     spread

     on your almost eternal

     turn

and on the matter the turn takes-on as it is turned by that

     matter—Earth—as

     my mind lags yet

     is always

on you, and the lag is part of the turn, its gold lip

     less than an

     arm's length from me

     now so that I

     can dip my fingers right out

     into it

     as we

     orbit the

     oval hoop and

the silence in here is staggering—

     how huge you

     carrying

me are—and there is

     never hurry—

     and nothing will posit

     you as

you carry the positors—as you carry the bottom

     of the river and its

     top and the clouds

on its top, watery, weak, and the clouds one looks up to

     to see

     as they too

     turn—

and you are not hunted—not hunting—not

hungry—

and you want

no

thing—are almost mute—(this is to be

considered)—

and the churchbells in

this of your

time zones (to praise what

exactly) begin,

and to

one place heavy

rains are

coming now,

and a horse

is riding wildly through one of your

darknesses,

its horseman praying fiercely

to get there

in time,

to that some-

where

else which is you, still you, only you,

in which only he

could be

for all eternity

too late.

V

LAPSE

(Summer Solstice, 1983, Iowa City)

It is entirely in my hands now as it returns like blood to remind me—

the chains so soft from wear, in my right, in my left—

the first time I, trying for perfection, of balance, of symmetry,

strap your twenty two pounds of eyes, blood, hair, bone—so recently inside me—

into the swing—and the sun still in the sky though it being so late

as I look up to see where this small package is to go

sent up by these two hands into the evening that won't stop

won't lower as it should into the gloam is it going to last forever,

and the grace that I feel at the center of my palms

as if my hands were leaves and light were coursing through

some hole in their grasp, the machine of time coming in,

as chlorophyll could—I was not yet so tired of believing—

I was still in the very beginning of being human,

the thing no one can tell another—he didn't find

what he searched for, she didn't understand what she

desired—the style of the story being the very wind

which comes up now as I glide down the chains

to the canvas bucket to pull you to me,

eyes closed as your eyes close, and for the first time in this lifetime

lift you back and up as far as I can, as high as I can,

then let you collapse so suddenly as I push you away from me,

with more force than gravity as I summon from within

what I try to feel is an accurate amount, a right fraction, of my strength,

not too much promise, not too much greed or ambition

or sense of beginning or capacity for dream—no—just

the amount to push you by that corresponds to pity,

who knows how to calculate that strong firm force,

as if I were sending a message forth that has to be delivered

and the claimant expects it, one of so many,

accompanied by my prayer that you be spared

from anything at all, from everything, and of course also its opposite,

that everything happen to you in large sheets of experience

as I tug back the chain-ends and push you out

telling you to *put out your legs and pump*

although you do not know what I am saying

as you have not yet spoken your first word,

not yet on that day that seems even now it will never end

as you come back to me and I catch you and this time of course

as I am human I push a little harder

as if the news I was shouting-out had not quite been heard,

as if the next push were the real one the one that asks for

the miracle—will I live or die if I pick this fruit

as it is sent back to my waiting hands and this time

it's stronger, the *yes* is taking over, your yes and my yes and our

greed to overcome *what,* into this first-ever solstice

with you in the born world,

let no one dare pick this fruit I think

as I cast the roundness of you up again now so high

into a mouth of sky agape yet without wonder

as if it eats everything and anything and does not know what day is

or time—this is *our* time—or that this next-on meal is being fed it,

as just under you the oval puddle from the recent rain lies

in the worn declivity where each one before you

has dug in her feet to push off or to stop—

and in it you flash as you go by

giving me for that instant an eye you its iris blinking,

the crucible of a blink in the large unflinching eye,

eye opened by the hundreds of small hopes taking on gravity at push-off,

and then the fatigue when for all the pumping and rising,

and how you could see over the tops of the houses,

up and over to where your own house is down there—

and the housing development, and the millions of leaves, and the slower children

                                        lagging behind

on the small road beneath—until the world stills,

and you alone are life, a huge bloom, a new force entering—

how then—even then—the sensation of *enough*

swarms, and *thought* or something like it, resumes,

and your mind is again in your hard grip

on the chains which had been until then as if unknown to your body

during what might have been the interglacial lull,

or the period during which the original ooze grew single-cell organisms,

which grew small claws and feet and then had to have eyes,

till your hands become again hard, heavy, and all

the yearning re-enters you as *lifetime,*

and your feet learn to brake

by scratching the ground a bit more each time—

and that is where the eye comes from,

the final oscillations, the desire to be done with vision,

what this morning's rain reminds us is still there beneath us

in an earth that will only swallow us entire

no matter what we push into it as here you and I again and again redo

the moment nine months ago you first began

to push and cry-out into the visible world.

It is here with me today in this hand grasping this pen

the weight of my transmission of force into you

the weight of catching you the first few times

the slow disappearance of your flesh from mine

as you hardly need a push when the centrifuge takes hold

and I just tap you a bit to keep you going

and we both feel the chains each in our own way

as they permit you to see over the given you shall never enter

no matter how long time is—never—

that gash you create in the evening air at your highest,

your own unique opening

which you can never fill,

cannot ever crawl back through and out,

except when that one moment comes and it will open and you will go,

once and once only and then, yes, you will.

I brought you in here I think in the evening,

in the grass and the town and the blinking windows,

in the dozens of lowering suns circling us in them.

MESSAGE FROM ARMAGH CATHEDRAL 2011

How will it be
told, this evidence, our life, all the clues missing? The clock I left in my hotel
room, all time landing on it at once, has no way to move forward so

round and round it
goes, making its ball its in-
visible

thread pulling through everything, tensile, on which the whole story

depends. But what if
it has no
direction. We,
whoever we

were, made that

up. Everything
that caught our
eye—shining—we

took. Because it exhibited unexpected movement, quicksilver, we took it by spear.
Because it whistled through air, barely dropping its aim from the sniper we

took it to
heart. Because it
lowered its
head in
shyness where sun
touched it and it

put one hand into its other and sang to itself thinking itself alone, we took it to

love, ob-
sessed, heavy
with

jealousy. Maybe we killed it to keep it. But yes it was love. Or we looked up and
thought "do we hear clearly?" and thought "yes" and went back to work. So then

why are *you* here today on this church floor in Armagh, piece of

stone, large as an infant,

hundreds of

pounds, triangular

body which ends at

waist, swaddled by

carvings, 3000 years

old, worked through

by chisel and wind

and porous where

granite has lost all

surface? I

crouch down and put my own pale arms round you. No one sees me. No one on
planet earth sees us. You say *who are you to me.* I see around you the animals run
into the woods for cover, away from the priest arriving, the sanctuary around
you tall, the shadows long, movement in it yes, human movement rare. You
must have sat in a high place I say here on the floor in this back

corner where you

are dis-

carded. W*hat have you seen* I say under my breath *that I might have seen.* I have
seen what is under your breath you reply. I press you to me as I did my child,
keeping my hand on the top of your head, your face on my chest. *Rainbow* you say.
Blood. Wind. Sky blue—though maybe not the same as yours now, no. There is a wedding

rehearsal in

the body of

the church—

laughter and constant

rehearsal of

vows—will you take her—I listen for the yes—will you take

him—the families

chattering, casual dress, no one in tears as these are not the real vows yet.
Tomorrow they will be cast in stone. Tomorrow they will vow to love for all eternity,
or that part of it they inhabit called "as long as you shall live," adding their sliver
of time onto the back of the beast turning under us. And the little girls coming round

for hide and seek. The men discussing politics. The women in the hum of long

time and short time. No one to stop the minutes. Their current cannot be

stanched. Soon it will be Fall again. The dress, she says, will have an old fashioned

cut. I wish her luck

when our paths cross

about an hour

from now. I mean

what I say to

the stranger. She sees me mean it. On the threshold. Each headed for our car. But you,

here on the floor, found in a garden in Tandragee, carved by someone with

strong hands in the Bronze Age, you are the ancient Irish king Nuadha, ruler of the

Tuatha Dé Danann, your people, for whom you lost your left arm, those you

defeated moving on elsewhere, westward, while you were forced to stand down

as king,

not being

"completely whole in

body, without

arm." And no good king

succeeded you. And after great hardship your people prayed your physician

Dian Cécht build

a new arm

out of silver

that you be able to

take up

kingship again.

Here you are holding the left arm on at shoulder with your right. Here you are whole

again. Almost. I bring my hand down onto that spot. Three hands, same

size, where I clasp yours, where I cover it, where I hold your arm on you

with you. At this

moment on this

earth mostly in desert many arms are not recovered after the device goes

off and the

limbs sever. Field

hospitals hold young men screaming where are my legs. Elsewhere leaders are making

                                                    decisions.

They are thinking about something else while they make them. And names are

                                                    called out by

a surgeon. An aide enters a room when called. A mother opens a door when called.

A child opens a gift when told ok, now, go ahead. A sentence is being pronounced: you

                                                    shall lose your

                                                    hands, you

                                                    shall lose your

feet. You might be a country. You might be a young man who touched the face of

a girl in a village thinking yourself alone. You are not alone the spies survive.

The spies are intact. They slaughter the whole animal for sacrifice, all of it at once.

The sentence is truncated even if the man is told: *do you have anything to say*

                                                    before we begin—

they do not wait for him to finish. His mouth hangs open over his swinging body.

His lifespan is missing a part: the future. His dream is missing a part: the rest. He is

                                                    missing his

extremity. Look, look, a button is missing on your long garment, lord. Look, the

jug of water has been brought to wash off the gaping place which is the redrawn

                                                    border to your

nation. I put my arms around you. You are the size of my child at six months. I put

my hand in your wide carved mouth: your maker made you speaking, or pro-

nouncing a law, or crying out—I can put my fingers into your stone mouth up to

my palm. Suckle. Speak. Cry. Promise. I will keep my fingers between your strong

                                                    cold lips you shall not be

alone. When I move up your cheeks I feel the bulge of your granite eyes, wide

brow, your eyes again, both hands with fingers rounding eyes. How shall we be

                                                    whole. Who

will make the missing part. The biggest obstacle is not knowing *of what?* Once I saw

a wall with its executions still in it—the bullet holes with my fingers in them were

                                                    just this eye's

size. Once I met you, you lowered your other arm and said why are you

                                                    taking me this way.

I said I am just on the road, we do not have another way to go. Where does the road go. Tell me, you said. I said hold your arm on I can't see a thing without its shine. This isn't a road. I saw bodies and statues but did not tell you. You were the thing I was here to get, to get to the place where the next king would take us. The last thing that dies? The last thing that dies is the body. I am feeling inside your

mouth. She is trying

to say the vow again—till death do us part—and I cannot make out what it is that time will do to them. Why are we going this way. The flowergirls are carrying a pretend

train now, laughter

as they go by. The ring bearer is carrying the pillow with no ring. In late morning a

short time before

the explosive device hidden in the basket of fresh laundry went off, Private Jackson,

who still had arms then,

reached down in secret, weapon in one hand, to feel the clean fabric. Actually

to smell it. *Clean,* he

thought. He used to hang it out for his mom, afternoons, hands up at the shoulders

of each shirt, an

extra clip in his teeth, as if surrendering. He remembers the lineup of shirtsleeves

all blowing one way

in the early evening, in Indiana, and for a blinding moment he realizes they had been

pointing, his

brothers, his father, his uncle, they all had been pointing—in their blues and whites

and checks. He

wishes he had turned to see, is what he thinks just before it goes off, they seemed

about to start a

dance—the tiny rhythm in the flapping sleeves. They did not seem like strangers.

Then he realizes it

is here now, that sound, is feet all running on dirt as fast as possible away from

this place.

The bride

steps out into the sun. I feel there is something I must tell her. May your wishes

come true I say,

guidebook in hand. Tomorrow, she says. I can't wait until tomorrow.